D0289581

The Pocket Book of
AFFIRMATIONS

The Pocket Book of AFFIRMATIONS

Positive words for a happy life

SIRIUS

SIRIUS

This edition published in 2019 by Sirius Publishing, a division of
Arcturus Publishing Limited,
26/27 Bickels Yard, 151–153 Bermondsey Street,
London SE1 3HA

Copyright © Arcturus Holdings Limited

All rights reserved. No part of this publication may be reproduced,
stored in a retrieval system, or transmitted, in any form or by any
means, electronic, mechanical, photocopying, recording or otherwise,
without written permission in accordance with the provisions of the
Copyright Act 1956 (as amended). Any person or persons who do
any unauthorised act in relation to this publication may be liable to
criminal prosecution and civil claims for damages.

ISBN: 978-1-78950-001-1
AD006849UK

Printed in China

Keep your face
to the sunshine
and you cannot
see the shadow.

Helen Keller

I am in charge of
how I feel today,
and I am choosing
happiness.

Love yourself. It is important to
stay positive because beauty
comes from the inside out.

Jenn Proske

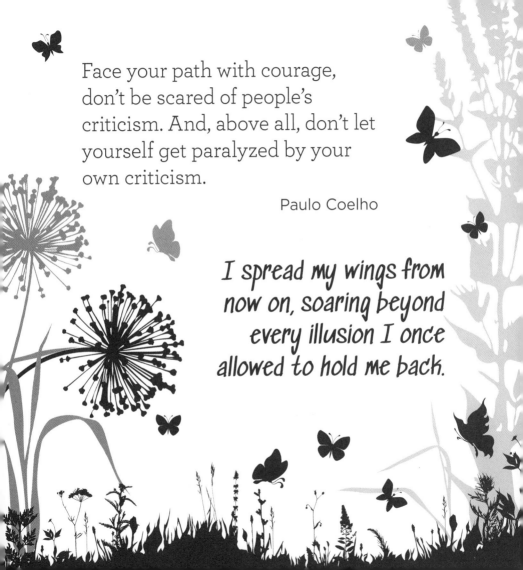

Face your path with courage, don't be scared of people's criticism. And, above all, don't let yourself get paralyzed by your own criticism.

Paulo Coelho

I spread my wings from now on, soaring beyond every illusion I once allowed to hold me back.

No one else is you, and
that is your power.

YOU CANNOT SWIM FOR NEW
HORIZONS UNTIL YOU HAVE COURAGE
TO LOSE SIGHT OF THE SHORE.

William Faulkner

Courage, in the final analysis, is nothing but an affirmative answer to the shocks of existence.

Kurt Goldstein

It is always easier to believe than to deny. Our minds are naturally affirmative.

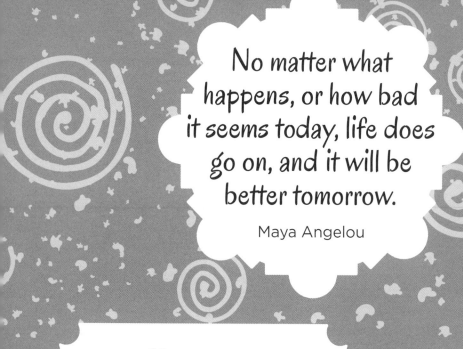

No matter what happens, or how bad it seems today, life does go on, and it will be better tomorrow.

Maya Angelou

I will continue to learn and grow.

THE AFFIRMATIVE OF AFFIRMATIVES . . . IS LOVE.

Ralph Waldo Emerson

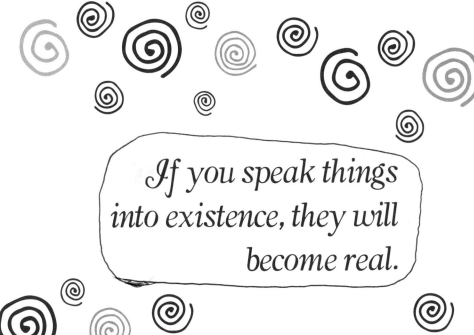

If you speak things into existence, they will become real.

If you get tired, learn
to rest, not to quit.

Banksy

*Your time is way too
valuable to be wasting on
people that can't accept
who you are.*

Turcois Ominek

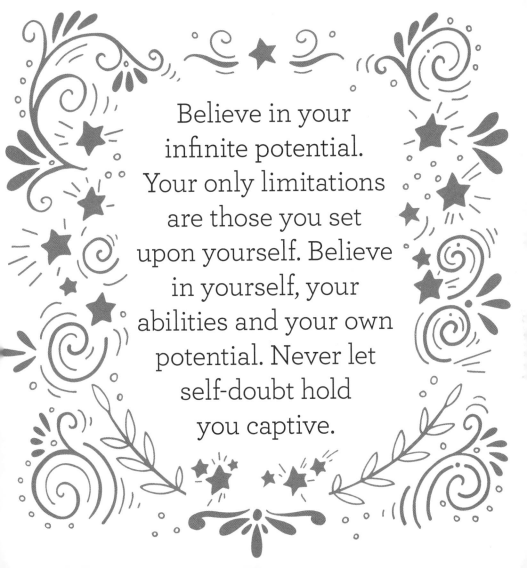

Believe in your infinite potential. Your only limitations are those you set upon yourself. Believe in yourself, your abilities and your own potential. Never let self-doubt hold you captive.

I AM THE ONLY ME THERE IS.
I AM WORTH THE TIME, EFFORT
AND DEDICATION THAT ARE
NECESSARY TO SUCCEED.

You are today where your
thoughts have brought you;
you will be tomorrow where
your thoughts take you.

James Allen

Stay away from
negative people –
they have a problem
for every solution.

Albert Einstein

*Limits exist only
in the mind.*

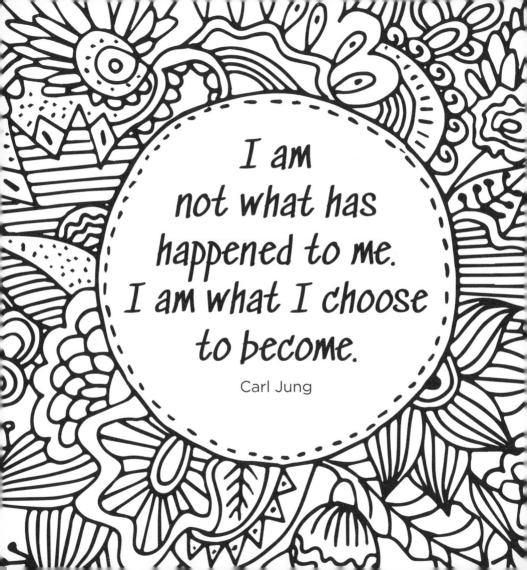

I am
not what has
happened to me.
I am what I choose
to become.

Carl Jung

Mistakes are a stepping stone to success. They are the path I must tread to achieve my dreams.

When you start living the life of your dreams, there will always be obstacles, doubters, mistakes and setbacks along the way. But with hard work, perseverance and self-belief, there is no limit to what you can achieve.

Roy T. Bennett

I have fun with all my endeavours,
even the most mundane.

Dare to believe that there is something better for you and that you can change your future and make it better.

Stephen Richards

I TRUST MYSELF AND KNOW MY INNER
WISDOM IS MY BEST GUIDE.

Don't pretend
to be what you're not;
instead, pretend to be
what you want to be.
It's not pretence, it is
a journey to
self-realization.

Michael Bassey Johnson

You don't have to know where you're going to get exactly where you need to go.

Marilyn A. Hepburn

I find joy and pleasure in the simple things in life.

Like seeds planted in the depths of our souls, our dreams are at the centre of who we really are. Our mission and our right is to nurture them and to allow them to grow. To follow your dreams takes courage, action, persistence, time and patience, but most of all you must first believe in them.

Melia Keeton-Digby

I rest in happiness when I go to sleep, knowing all is well in my world.

Whatever you did today is enough.
Whatever you felt today is valid.
Whatever you thought today isn't to be judged.
Repeat the above.

Brittany Burgunder

I shall no longer allow negative thoughts or feelings to drain me of my energy. Instead I shall focus on all the good that is in my life. I will think it, feel it and speak it. By doing so, I will send out vibes of positive energy into the world and I shall be grateful for all the wonderful things it will attract into my life.

The best option to take will be the one that scares you the most. It is the one that requires you to go deeper than you have ever gone before. Your mind may tell you it's not a good idea and bring up all the reasons why it won't work, but check your heart. Intuitively, if it feels right, it is right.

Susan Samaroo

Stand for something.
Make your life mean something.
Start where you are with what
you have. You are enough.

Germany Kent

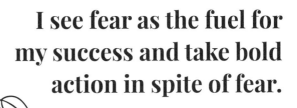

I see fear as the fuel for
my success and take bold
action in spite of fear.

There will be haters, there will be doubters, there will be non-believers; and then there will be you, proving them wrong.

Jennifer van Allen

I FEEL POWERFUL, CAPABLE, CONFIDENT, ENERGETIC, AND ON TOP OF THE WORLD.

Oh yes, the past can hurt. But you can either run from it or learn from it.

Rafiki

I will surround myself with positive people who will bring out the best in me.

Be careful how you are talking to yourself, because you are listening.

Lisa M. Hayes

To believe in yourself is to light a spark with the potential to start a fire.

Richelle E. Goodrich

I choose to be unstoppable. I am bigger than my concerns and worries. The strength of others inspires me daily. I focus on my goal. I trust my intuition and live a courageous life.

I can – and I will.

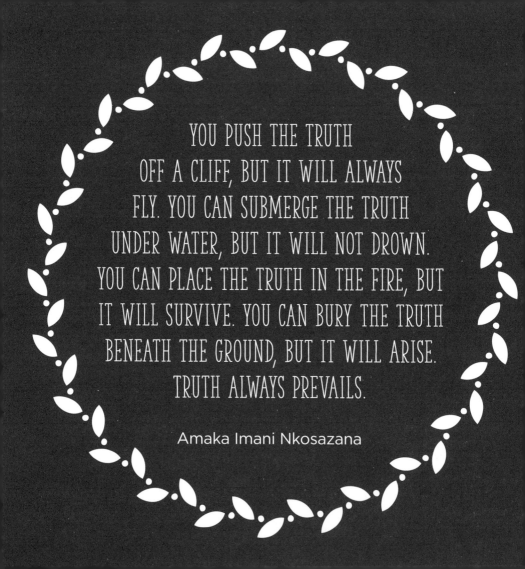

YOU PUSH THE TRUTH OFF A CLIFF, BUT IT WILL ALWAYS FLY. YOU CAN SUBMERGE THE TRUTH UNDER WATER, BUT IT WILL NOT DROWN. YOU CAN PLACE THE TRUTH IN THE FIRE, BUT IT WILL SURVIVE. YOU CAN BURY THE TRUTH BENEATH THE GROUND, BUT IT WILL ARISE. TRUTH ALWAYS PREVAILS.

Amaka Imani Nkosazana

I have integrity. I am totally reliable. I do what I say.

Whatever you think you can do or believe you can do, begin it. Action has magic, grace and power in it.

Sally Brampton

I ENJOY EXERCISING MY BODY AND STRENGTHENING MY MUSCLES.

With every breath out,
I release stress from my body.

Break your shackles and reach out to your freedom. Break to pieces whatever indoctrination and programming that holds you hostage. The world is yours. Get possession of it.

Bangambiki Habyarimana

I want to live my life to its fullest potential. I want to embrace my own purpose, however large or small it may be. I want to find my own Nehru moments and take positive steps toward becoming the person I am meant to be. The journey will undoubtedly be a winding one, filled with surprises and setbacks as well as gifts. But I'm ready to embrace it fully, wherever it may take me.

Mallika Chopra

If you must walk in someone's shadow, make sure it's your own.

Rasheed Ogunlaru

SELF-CONFIDENCE IS THE FOUNDATION OF ALL GREAT SUCCESS AND ACHIEVEMENT.

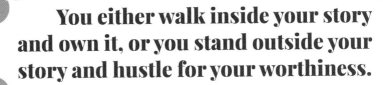

You either walk inside your story and own it, or you stand outside your story and hustle for your worthiness.

Brené Brown

I make my own choices and I create my own future.

Your worth as a person does not depend on how well you succeed, what you accomplish, or what other people think of you.

I came to the conclusion that there is an existential moment in your life when you must decide to speak for yourself. Nobody else can speak for you.

Martin Luther King Jr.

Don't measure your progress using someone else's ruler.

MY UNPLEASANT PAST HAS GIVEN
ME WISDOM TO BUILD
A PLEASANT FUTURE.

Sheldon Pereira

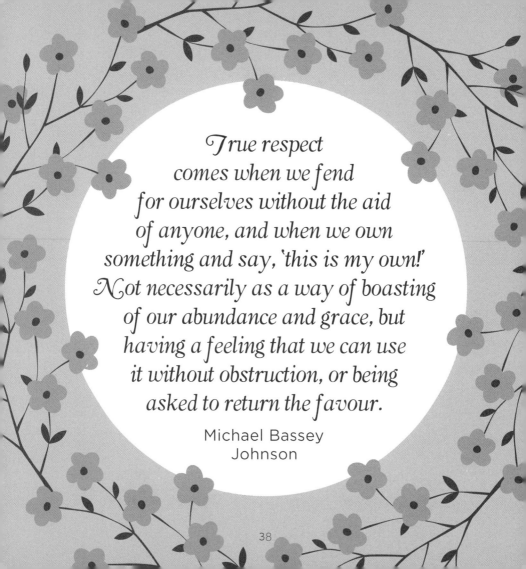

*True respect
comes when we fend
for ourselves without the aid
of anyone, and when we own
something and say, 'this is my own!'
Not necessarily as a way of boasting
of our abundance and grace, but
having a feeling that we can use
it without obstruction, or being
asked to return the favour.*

Michael Bassey
Johnson

I pay attention and listen to what my body needs for health and vitality.

SHE LOOKED AT THE GIRL IN THE MIRROR AND THE GIRL IN THE MIRROR LOOKED BACK AT HER. I WILL BE BRAVE, THOUGHT CORALINE. NO, I *AM* BRAVE.

Neil Gaiman

I find deep inner
peace within myself
as I am.

SOMETIMES IT IS THE PEOPLE WHO NO ONE
IMAGINES ANYTHING OF WHO DO THE THINGS
THAT NO ONE CAN IMAGINE.

Christopher Morcom

**I release past anger and hurts
and fill myself with serenity
and peaceful thoughts.**

*Trust what you know; have faith
in where you go; if there's no
wind, row; or go with the flow.*

Ed Parrish III

Someone who sees the invisible can do the impossible.

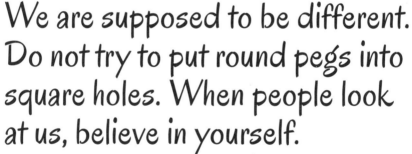

We are supposed to be different. Do not try to put round pegs into square holes. When people look at us, believe in yourself.

Manoj Arora

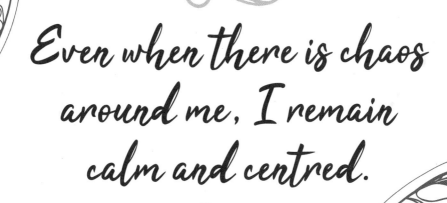

Even when there is chaos around me, I remain calm and centred.

I HAVE TO LEARN TO FIND THAT INNER
CORE OF STRENGTH THAT I AM DEFINITELY
MADE UP OF, AND STRETCH IT INTO AREAS
WHERE I DON'T ALWAYS USE IT.

Jodie Andrefski

My world is a peaceful,
loving and joy-filled place.

I accept myself, even
though I sometimes
make mistakes.

Don't be afraid of losing your friends and followers. Be afraid of losing yourself to the world, because you settled for the opinions of others.

Joel Brown

The question isn't who is going to let me; it's who is going to stop me?

Ayn Rand

Successful people build one another up. They motivate, inspire and push one another. Unsuccessful people just hate, blame and complain.

This life is what you make it. No matter what, you're going to mess up sometimes. But the good part is you get to decide how you're going to mess it up and how you will make it better!

Marilyn Monroe

A river cuts through a rock not because of its power, but its persistence.

If you want to change the world, go home and love your family.

Mother Teresa

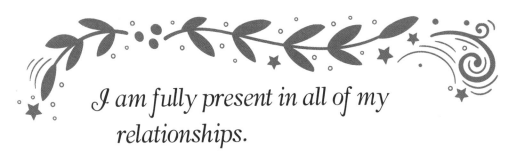

I am fully present in all of my relationships.

∘ ∘ • •

My home is a peaceful sanctuary where I feel safe and happy.

∘ • ∘ •

THE SOUL SHOULD ALWAYS STAND AJAR,
READY TO WELCOME THE ECSTATIC EXPERIENCE.

Emily Dickinson

In life, you will realize that there is a role for everyone you meet. Some will test you, some will use you, some will love you, and some will teach you. But the ones who are important are the ones who bring out the best in you. They're the rare and amazing people who remind you why it's worth it.

Never be bullied into silence. Never allow yourself to be made a victim. Accept no one's definition of your life; define yourself.

Robert Frost

Courage is fire, and bullying is smoke.

Benjamin Disraeli

It is better to be hated
for who you are than to be
loved for someone you're not.
It's a sign of your worth
sometimes, if you're hated
by the right people.

Bette Davis

When there is nothing
left to say, lift your head up
high, smile, and walk away.

WHAT WE INSTIL IN OUR CHILDREN WILL BE THE FOUNDATION UPON WHICH THEY BUILD THEIR FUTURE.

Steve Maraboli

My job as a mother is to protect my children from anything and everything. If that means eliminating people from our lives – even family – then so be it.

When some things go wrong, take a moment to be thankful for the many more things that are still going right.

Each morning, when I open my eyes, I say to myself: I, not events, have the power to make me happy or unhappy today. I can choose which it shall be.

Groucho Marx

Raise your standards
and the universe will
meet you there.

Have the courage to follow your heart and
intuition. They somehow already know
what you truly want to become.
Everything else is secondary.

Steve Jobs

Instead of worrying about what you cannot control, shift your energy to what you can create.

Roy T. Bennett

You can, you should, and if you're brave enough to start, you will.

Stephen King

Don't let your struggle become your identity.

Every experience in my life has shaped me to be where I am at this very moment. I am exactly who I am supposed to be.

There are so many beautiful reasons to be happy.

We can complain because rose bushes have thorns, or rejoice because thorns have roses.

Alphonse Karr

Make yourself a priority.

FEAR LESS, HOPE MORE; EAT LESS, CHEW MORE; WHINE LESS, BREATHE MORE; TALK LESS, SAY MORE; LOVE MORE, AND ALL GOOD THINGS WILL BE YOURS.

Swedish proverb

A CALM MIND BRINGS INNER STRENGTH AND SELF-CONFIDENCE, SO THAT'S VERY IMPORTANT FOR GOOD HEALTH.

Strive for progress, not perfection.

Life isn't about finding yourself; it's about creating yourself.

You may have a fresh start any moment you choose, for this thing we call 'failure' is not the falling down, but the staying down.

Mary Pickford

Today you are you,
That is truer than true.
There is no one alive
Who is youer than you.

Dr Seuss

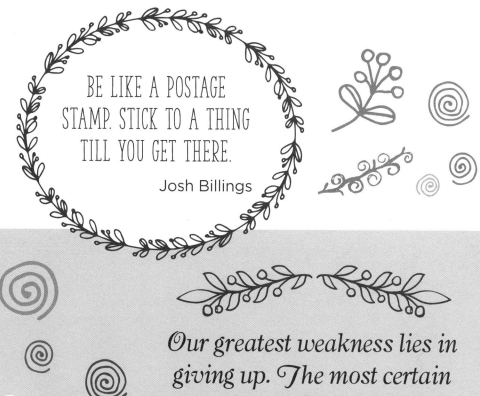

BE LIKE A POSTAGE
STAMP. STICK TO A THING
TILL YOU GET THERE.

Josh Billings

Our greatest weakness lies in giving up. The most certain way to succeed is always to try just one more time.

If you look the right way,
you can see that the
whole world is a garden.

Frances Hodgson Burnett

Don't cry over the past – it's
gone. Don't stress about the future
– it hasn't arrived. Live in the
present, and make it beautiful.

There is no elevator
to success.
You have to take
the stairs.

The harder you work,
the luckier you get.

Gary Player

If there is light in the soul, there will be beauty in the person.

Be faithful to that which exists within yourself.

André Gide

I am thankful for all of those who said NO to me. It's because of them I'm doing it myself.

Albert Einstein

We rise by lifting others.

Avoid negative people at all costs. They tire you out and wear you down.

Brian Tracy

When the wrong people leave your life, the right things start happening.

Eat like you love yourself.
Move like you love yourself.
Speak like you love yourself.
Act like you love yourself.

There are two types of people who will tell you that you cannot make a difference in this world: those who are afraid to try and those who are afraid you will succeed.

Ray Goforth

Open-minded people embrace being wrong, are free of illusions, don't mind what people think of them, and question everything – even themselves.

No one outside ourselves can rule us inwardly. When we know this, we become free.

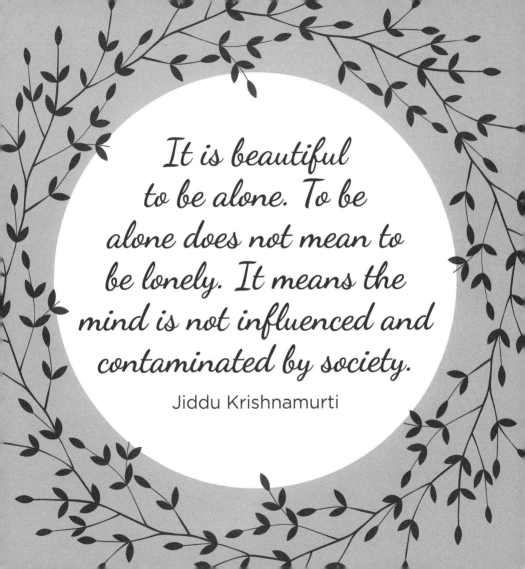

It is beautiful
to be alone. To be
alone does not mean to
be lonely. It means the
mind is not influenced and
contaminated by society.

Jiddu Krishnamurti

Standing alone doesn't mean I'm alone. It means I am strong enough to handle things all by myself.

Seek the wisdom of the ages, but look at the world through the eyes of a child.

Ron Wild

Once you've accepted your flaws, no one can use them against you. You are YOU, and that's the beginning and the end – no apologies, no regrets.

What we see depends mainly on what we look for.

John Lubbock

Don't tell people your plans. Show them your results.

TRUE FREEDOM IS ALWAYS SPIRITUAL.
IT HAS SOMETHING TO DO WITH YOUR INNERMOST
BEING, WHICH CANNOT BE CHAINED, HANDCUFFED,
OR PUT INTO A JAIL.

Rajneesh

The fool doth think he is wise, but the wise man knows himself to be a fool.

William Shakespeare

Education is the passport to the future, for tomorrow belongs to those who prepare for it today.

Malcolm X

Learning gives creativity.
Creativity leads to thinking.
Thinking provides knowledge.
Knowledge makes you great.

Abdul Kalam

Wrong is wrong, even if everyone is doing it. Right is right, even if only you are doing it.

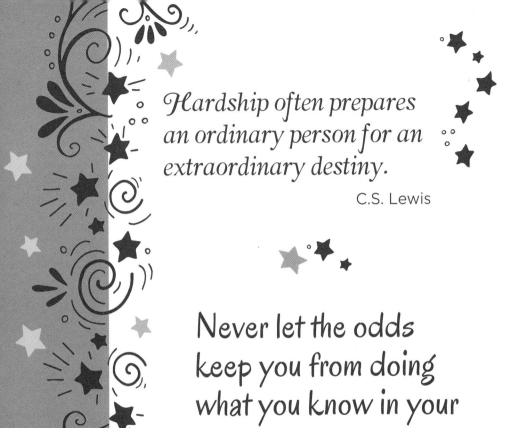

*Hardship often prepares
an ordinary person for an
extraordinary destiny.*

C.S. Lewis

Never let the odds
keep you from doing
what you know in your
heart you were meant
to do.

A positive attitude will not solve all your problems, but it will annoy enough people to make it worth the effort.

Herm Albright

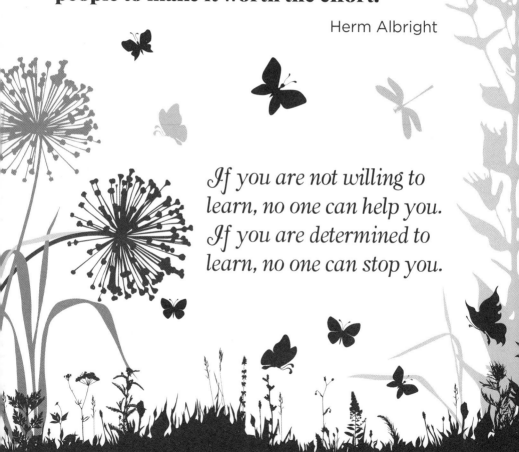

If you are not willing to learn, no one can help you. If you are determined to learn, no one can stop you.

Do stuff. Be clenched, curious. Not waiting for inspiration's shove or society's kiss on your forehead. Pay attention. It's all about paying attention. Attention is vitality. It connects you with others. It makes you eager. Stay eager.

Susan Sontag

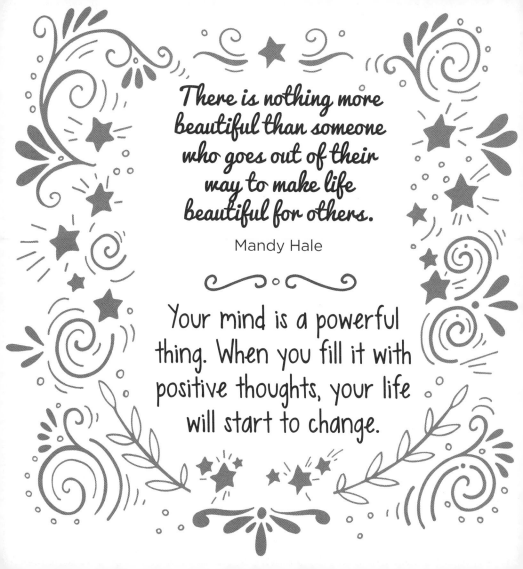

There is nothing more beautiful than someone who goes out of their way to make life beautiful for others.

Mandy Hale

Your mind is a powerful thing. When you fill it with positive thoughts, your life will start to change.

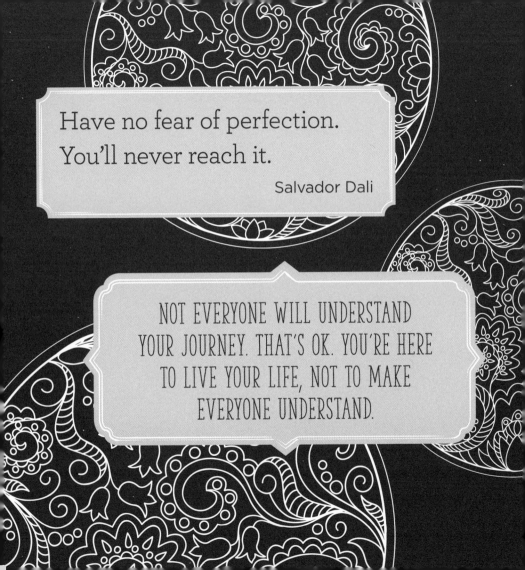

Have no fear of perfection.
You'll never reach it.

Salvador Dali

NOT EVERYONE WILL UNDERSTAND
YOUR JOURNEY. THAT'S OK. YOU'RE HERE
TO LIVE YOUR LIFE, NOT TO MAKE
EVERYONE UNDERSTAND.

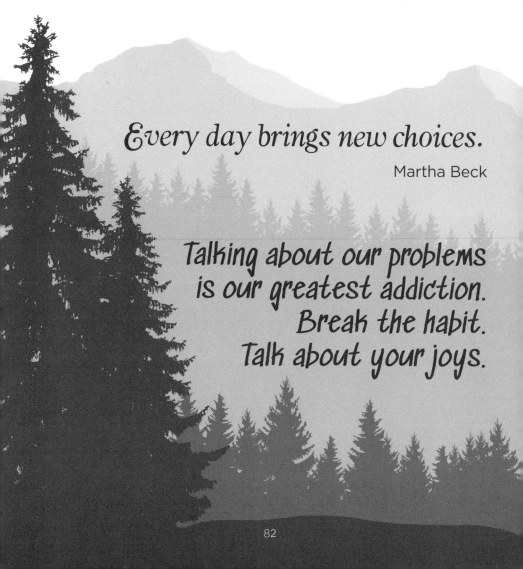

Every day brings new choices.

Martha Beck

Talking about our problems
is our greatest addiction.
Break the habit.
Talk about your joys.

Sometimes you just have to turn the page to realize there's more to your book of life than the page you're stuck on. Don't try to fix what's been broken in your past, let your future create something better.

LIFE ISN'T ABOUT WAITING FOR THE STORM TO PASS. IT'S ABOUT LEARNING HOW TO DANCE IN THE RAIN.

I'm always doing things I can't do. That's how I get to do them.

Pablo Picasso

If you want something you never had, you have to do something you've never done.

I have an everyday religion that works for me. Love yourself first and everything else falls into line.

Lucille Ball

In the long run, you hit what you aim at — so aim high.

Henry David Thoreau

If opportunity doesn't knock, build a door.

Milton Berle

Life is not about how fast you run or how high you climb, but how well you bounce.

The positive thinker sees the invisible, feels the intangible, and achieves the impossible.

An arrow can only be shot by pulling it backwards. So when life is dragging you back with difficulties, it means that it's going to launch you into something great. So just focus, and keep aiming.

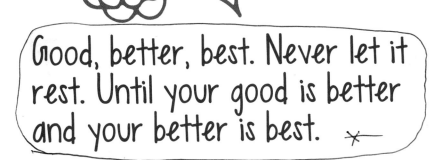

Good, better, best. Never let it rest. Until your good is better and your better is best. ✕—

Never apologize for having high standards. People who really want to be in your life will rise up to meet them.

With the new day comes new strength and new thoughts.

Eleanor Roosevelt

Exist to be happy, not to impress.

90

A HIGH STATION IN
LIFE IS EARNED BY THE
GALLANTRY WITH WHICH
APPALLING EXPERIENCES ARE
SURVIVED WITH GRACE.

Tennessee Williams

Live your life and
forget your age.

The ones who say 'you can't' and 'you won't' are probably the ones scared that 'you will'.

Be clearly aware of the stars and infinity on high. Then life seems almost enchanted after all.

Vincent van Gogh

TO BE THE BEST, YOU MUST BE
ABLE TO HANDLE THE WORST.

It took a lot of courage to take the
high road, but I would rather be
significant with six million people
watching a show with meaning,
than everyone watching a show
with no meaning.

Oprah Winfrey

Impossible only means that you haven't found the solution yet.

Challenges are what make life interesting and overcoming them is what makes life meaningful.

Joshua J. Marine

Live each day as if your life had just begun.

Johann Wolfgang von Goethe

Rock bottom became the solid foundation on which I rebuilt my life.

J.K. Rowling

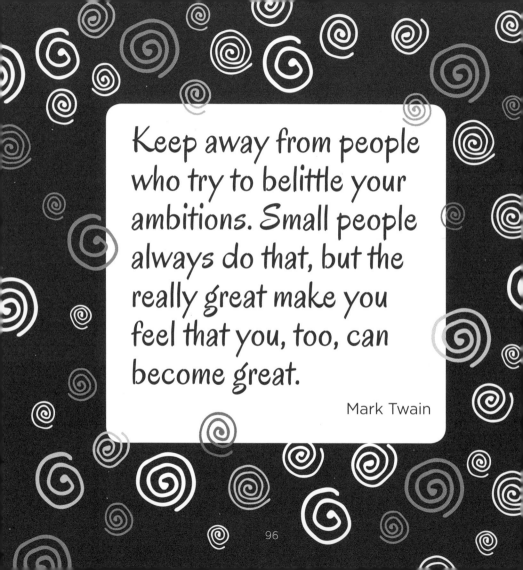

Keep away from people who try to belittle your ambitions. Small people always do that, but the really great make you feel that you, too, can become great.

Mark Twain

A bend in the road is not the end of the road . . . unless you fail to make the turn.

Helen Keller

A thousand disappointments in the past cannot equal the power of one positive action right now. Go ahead and go for it.

I CAN And will succeed today in every way with peace and ease

Positive anything
is better than
negative nothing.

Elbert Hubbard

If you truly want
to change your
life, you must
first be willing to
change your mind.

The greatest discovery of any generation is that a human being can alter his life by altering his attitude.

William James

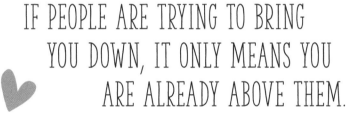

IF PEOPLE ARE TRYING TO BRING YOU DOWN, IT ONLY MEANS YOU ARE ALREADY ABOVE THEM.

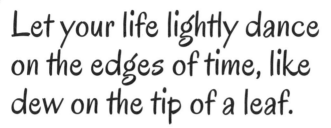

Let your life lightly dance
on the edges of time, like
dew on the tip of a leaf.

Rabindranath Tagore

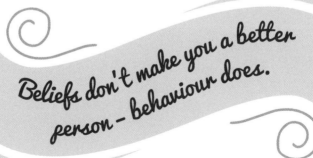

Beliefs don't make you a better person – behaviour does.

Don't tell me the sky's the limit when there are footprints on the moon.

It is always the simple that produces the marvellous.

Amelia Barr

I don't regret the things I've done, I regret the things I didn't do when I had the chance.

It is not living that matters, but living rightly.

Socrates

In every day, there are 1,440 minutes. That means we have 1,440 daily opportunities to make a positive impact.

Les Brown

Your children will become who you are, so be who you want them to be.

IF YOU'RE LUCKY
ENOUGH TO
BE DIFFERENT,
DON'T EVER CHANGE.

You must stand for something!
It does not have to be grand, but it
must be a positive that brings light
to someone else's darkness.

Anthony Carmona

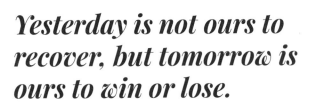

Yesterday is not ours to recover, but tomorrow is ours to win or lose.

Lyndon B. Johnson

Difficulties in your life don't come to destroy you, but to help you realize your hidden potential.

Nice days and nice people are fine, but what I really like are things that can be described as ferocious. Lightning storms and loud, booming thunder. People who don't apologize for being unique.

There are no failures in
life, only those who give
up too soon.

**You have to go wholeheartedly
into anything in order to
achieve anything worth having.**

Frank Lloyd Wright

EVERY HUMAN HAS SOMETHING TO OFFER THIS WORLD; THE QUESTION IS, WILL WE CREATE A SOCIETY THAT CAN SEE EVERYONE'S WORTH?

Michael T. Coe

To live a creative life, we must lose our fear of being wrong.

The meaning of life is to find your gift. The purpose of life is to give it away.

Black Lives Matter is really an affirmation for our people. It's a love note for our people, but it's also a demand. We know that the system was not designed for justice for us.

Opal Tometi

Humour is an affirmation of dignity, a declaration of man's superiority to all that befalls him.

Romain Gary

Running away from your problems is a race you'll never win.

A lot of the themes that I write about are an affirmation of our existence on Earth and making people feel like they are not alone, and making them feel like it is OK to be a little bit insane. That has always been sort of my credo in life.

Grace Potter

For me, diverse beauty is an affirmation of every single person in his or her own skin.

Philomena Kwao

Put your heart, mind and soul into even your smallest acts. This is the secret of success.

Swami Sivananda

Never give up on
something you really want.
It's difficult to wait,
but more difficult to regret.

YOU WILL NEVER BE BRAVE IF YOU DON'T
GET HURT. YOU WILL NEVER LEARN IF YOU
DON'T MAKE MISTAKES. YOU WILL NEVER BE
SUCCESSFUL IF YOU DON'T ENCOUNTER FAILURE.

There are two ways of spreading light: to be the candle or the mirror that reflects it.

Edith Wharton

I WILL LOVE THE LIGHT FOR IT SHOWS ME THE WAY, YET I WILL ENDURE THE DARKNESS BECAUSE IT SHOWS ME THE STARS.

Og Mandino

Don't write your name on sand; waves will wash it away. Don't write your name in the sky; wind may blow it away. Write your name in the hearts of people you come in touch with. That's where it will stay.

*You must do the things
you think you cannot do.*

Eleanor Roosevelt

IT'S THE REPETITION OF AFFIRMATIONS THAT
LEADS TO BELIEF. AND ONCE THAT BELIEF BECOMES
A DEEP CONVICTION, THINGS BEGIN TO HAPPEN.

Muhammad Ali

No matter what people tell you, words and ideas can change the world.

Robin Williams

A mistake should be your teacher, not your attacker. A mistake is a lesson, not a loss. It is a temporary, necessary detour, not a dead end.

MEMORIES OF OUR LIVES, OF OUR WORKS AND OUR DEEDS WILL CONTINUE IN OTHERS.

Rosa Parks

It doesn't matter if the glass is half empty or half full. Be thankful that you have a glass, and grateful that there's something in it.

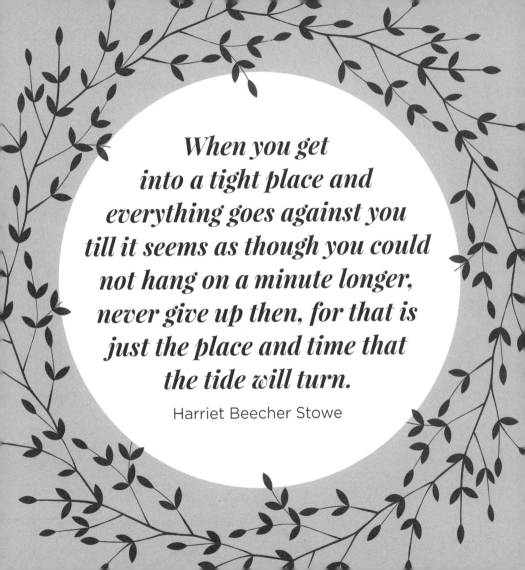

*When you get
into a tight place and
everything goes against you
till it seems as though you could
not hang on a minute longer,
never give up then, for that is
just the place and time that
the tide will turn.*

Harriet Beecher Stowe

When we seek to discover the best in others, we somehow bring out the best in ourselves.

William Arthur Ward

Always act like you're wearing an invisible crown.

Throw your dreams into space like a kite, and you do not know what it will bring back — a new life, a new friend, a new love, a new country.

Anais Nin

Train your mind to see the good in everything.

Expect nothing. Live frugally on surprise.

Alice Walker

SOME DAYS THERE WON'T BE A SONG IN YOUR HEART. SING ANYWAY.

Emory Austin

The real measure of your wealth is how much you'd be worth if you lost all your money.

Being happy doesn't mean that everything is perfect. It means that you've decided to look beyond the imperfections.

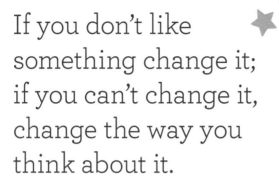

If you don't like
something change it;
if you can't change it,
change the way you
think about it.

Mary Engelbreit

Keep a green tree in your
heart, and perhaps a singing
bird will come.

Chinese proverb

If we try to see something positive in everything we do, life won't necessarily become easier but it becomes more valuable.

In the depth of winter, I finally learned that there was in me an invincible summer.

Albert Camus

Life is a shipwreck,
but we must
not forget to sing
in the lifeboats.

Voltaire

**Every day may not
be good, but there's
something good in
every day.**

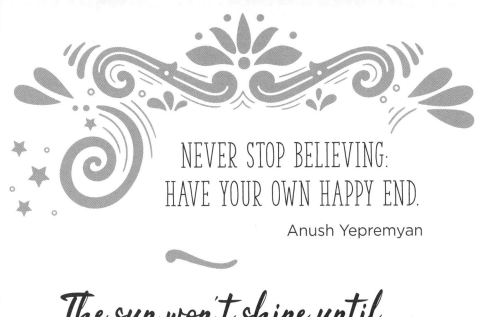

NEVER STOP BELIEVING:
HAVE YOUR OWN HAPPY END.

Anush Yepremyan

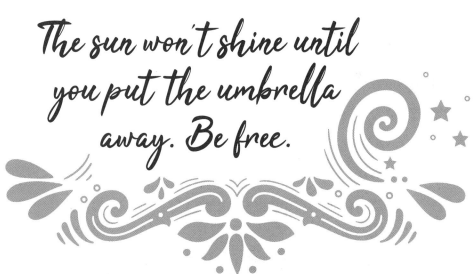

The sun won't shine until
you put the umbrella
away. Be free.

I thank you God for this most amazing day, for the leaping greenly spirits of trees, and for the blue dream of sky, and for everything which is natural, which is infinite, which is yes.

E.E. Cummings